SUGAR GLIDERS

THE ESSENTIAL GUIDE TO OWNERSHIP & CARE FOR YOUR PET

Kate H. Pellham

© 2015

DISCLAIMER

Edition v1.0 (15.11.26)

Table of Contents

Chapter 1: Introduction to Sugar Gliders

Sugar gliders are a nocturnal and arboreal marsupial thought to be native to Australia's rainforests, although they're also found in New Guinea, Tasmania, and some islands of Indonesia. Their scientific name is Petaurus breviceps, and though they may look like other small pets, they're more closely related to possums, wombats, and other marsupials. They are insectivores, not herbivores, meaning they eat predominantly insects when they're in the wild. The most unique and identifiable thing that marsupials have in common is their method of reproduction. Like kangaroos, female sugar gliders have a pouch where their joeys live for the first few weeks of life. Marsupials, generally, have a very short gestation period followed by a longer developmental period.

The scientific name of sugar gliders translates to roughly "short-headed rope-dancer." The "glider" in their common name also refers to their ability to glide from tree-top to tree-top. "Sugar," meanwhile, refers to their sweet tooth. When insects aren't as prevalent during the colder winter months, sugar gliders will eat the sap from eucalyptus and gum trees and the nectar of tropical flowers. They'll also eat manna, the hard crusty sap produced around wounds in tree trunks.

Physical appearance

A full-grown sugar glider has a body that's around 5-7 inches long, with a tail of approximately equal length, and should weigh about 4-6 ounces, with males generally bigger than females. Though they can be selectively bred for different colorations, their standard coat is dark gray and white, with a black stripe down its spine and extending over the top of its head. Most sugar gliders also have black markings on their face and tip of their tail. They have claws and opposable digits on both their front and hind feet, evolved for skillful climbing and grabbing wriggling bugs while they eat them. Their second and third toes on the back feet are syndactylous, meaning they're fused together—a single toe with two nails. This is a common feature of marsupials and is used by sugar gliders for grooming. Sugar glider eyes are large and solid black, and they have thin, hairless ears that twitch constantly to pick up sounds all around them.

One of a sugar glider's most distinctive features is the patagium, a thin membrane of skin stretching between the front and back legs. This allows them to glide from tree to tree for distances up to 100 meters. They use their tails as rudders to direct their gliding, and can even snatch insects out of mid-air during their glide. The technical term for this behavior is volplaning—it's a controlled glide, not a flight, meaning sugar gliders can't gain altitude while they're soaring except from external factors. Though this behavior seems very exotic to people living in North America, sugar gliders are one of several volplaning possums that live in Australia.

Behavior in the wild

Sugar gliders are social animals, living in colonies of up to 15 animals in the wild. This usually consists of 5-7 adults with their joeys. Colonies have a distinct social hierarchy, with a dominant alpha male who impregnates most of the females, though he'll occasionally allow a second male to mate within the colony if it's large enough. Once they've emerged from their pouches, most joeys will depart from their home colony and meet up with other juveniles in the wild to form their own offshoot colony. This instinctual drive to branch out helps to keep wild glider populations from becoming inbred. During times of plenty, offshoot colonies will sometimes re-join with their home colonies for a time, forming extended family groups of up to 30 individuals.

Sugar glider colonies nest in the hollows of tree trunks. Though they are capable of breeding year-round, most sugar gliders breed during the spring and summer when insects are plentiful. New joeys spend about 70 days in their mother's pouch before being left in the nest to finish growing. During colder, winter months, sugar gliders huddle together in their colony groups and share warmth. Rarely, when the temperature drops especially low, sugar gliders can enter a torpid state similar to hibernation, in which their heart rate, body temperature, and blood pressure drop for a few days to keep their systems running.

Behaviors and sounds

Sugar gliders use both verbal and non-verbal communication within their colonies. The sounds you're likely to hear as a sugar glider owner have very distinctive meanings, and learning the language of your pets will go a long way toward making your care thorough and effective.

The first few times you try to interact with your sugar gliders, you'll probably hear them crabbing. This distinctive sound is as hard to describe as it is unmistakable—it sounds sort of like a cross between a dolphin and an old-school modem. It's often accompanied by a defensive posture that's tensed with one leg raised. This sound means your sugar glider is scared and is ready to bite an intruder to defend its colony—and if that intruder is your hand, it's probably best to back off a little bit. In interactions with other sugar gliders, this sound can also mean the glider is defending its young or territory, or having a dominance squabble.

The other main sound you'll hear your sugar gliders make is barking. This is higher pitched than a dog bark, and sounds very similar to the sounds squirrels make. Barking is a general attempt to get the attention of colony mates. You may hear it when you enter the room around playtime—in this context, your glider's telling you where he is. It can also be a warning that there's something happening his cage mates should pay attention to, and you'll often see the rest of the animals in the colony freeze and look around when one of them starts to bark.

Sugar gliders occasionally hiss. Unlike cat hissing, this is not always a negative sound, and they seem to make it most often when they're foraging for food. You should only consider hissing to be cause for concern if your gliders make the sound while they're trying to go to the bathroom. This means they're experiencing some discomfort and may have a urinary tract infection or intestinal blockage. Clicks, chirps, sneezes, and purrs are also common noises, and generally mean your gliders are contented and peacefully interacting with their buddies.

Aside from the noises they make, sugar gliders rely heavily on scent to interact with their environment. New gliders will get to know each other by rubbing against each others scent glands. A sugar glider's scent is a personal signature akin to a fingerprint, though humans will rarely smell all but the strongest musk from un-neutered males. Females have scent glands near their genitals and pouch, while males have scent glands on their chest between their front legs and on the center of their forehead. In un-neutered males, the forehead scent gland often results in a diamond-shaped bald patch on the head.

Sugar gliders as pets

Sugar gliders have been captive bred in North America for about 15 years. This means that, while great strides have been made recently in understanding their unique dietary and environmental needs, sugar gliders are not domesticated in the same way as a cat or a dog. The animal's wild survival instincts are still very present. This is important to keep in mind especially as you're trying to train or discipline your animal. Negative reinforcement will not work with sugar gliders the same way it works with dogs. If you yell at your glider, he will only start to see you as a threat. Positive reinforcement—associating your smell and the behaviors you're looking for with comfort and safety through treats and soft words—will yield much better results.

Though they are not domesticated, sugar gliders can be tamed and do bond readily with their keepers. When raised correctly, they are loving and affectionate pets. It's important to keep in mind that there's no such thing as a "bad" sugar glider, only a glider who's exhibiting bad behavior—and since they're instinct-driven, the vast majority of the time these behaviors will have a cause, be it fear and discomfort over a change in surroundings, problems with the environment, or negative interactions with cage-mates, other people, or other pets. Like with other exotic animals, it works best to take a very animal-centric approach to sugar glider care. By doing your best to replicate their wild environment and respect their needs and autonomy, you will get the best out of your gliders.

Sugar gliders make great pets, but they are not the best pets for every household. The fact that they're nocturnal puts many people off. Some sugar gliders partially adapt to their human's diurnal lifestyle over time and may be awake and ready to play during daylight hours, but that doesn't mean they'll sleep quietly through the night. The crabbing and barking sounds described earlier can be pretty loud, and they'll be running around their cage and using their exercise wheel throughout the night. If noise at night isn't a concern, most keepers find their sugar glider's nocturnal schedule works great with their busy days. Your pets will be asleep while you're off at work or school, and will be just waking up and ready to eat and play around dusk, when you're settling down to dinner yourself.

As social animals, sugar gliders need other animals for companionship to stay healthy. They are not mentally equipped to live alone and solitary sugar gliders develop serious behavioral issues and potentially fatal health problems. They're also extremely active animals. Put together, these two facts translate to extremely large enclosures on the same scale as aviaries or iguana cages. For their own safety, sugar gliders must be kept in a sealed-off area at night—they're very inquisitive and intelligent, and even the safest human home has too many potential hazards for a sugar glider to roam without supervision. This makes them bad pets for apartments and other small living spaces. It also means they're difficult to transport, and aren't the best pet for lifestyles that call for frequent moves. If you travel frequently, you shouldn't expect to bring your sugar gliders with you, and will need to budget for pet sitters when estimating your expenses.

Sugar gliders live much longer than your typical small pet. The average lifespan is around 6 years in the wild, but in captivity they live an average of 9-10 years, and may live as long as 15. Most keepers see this as a good thing, but it does mean sugar gliders are a commitment. They're not an impulse pet and shouldn't be bought on a whim. If you buy a sugar glider for a child, keep in mind that the pet will probably still be alive when your kid goes off to college—and since there's no chance of a healthy cage fitting in a dorm room, his sugar glider will become your sugar glider.

In terms of their daily care, sugar gliders require a similar time commitment to a dog or a cat. Daily care includes preparing fresh food, cleaning the cage and litter pan, and letting the animals out for some play and exercise. If you don't think you'll have time to do all three of these things every day, it's not fair to the animal to bring it into your life. Also consider what sugar gliders eat. Insects like mealworms, crickets, and grasshoppers should be a regular part of your pet's diet. If bugs make you squeamish, sugar gliders might not be your best pet.

If all of this sounds reasonable to you, sugar gliders do have a lot of advantages as pets. They're very affectionate and playful animals and form tight, loving bonds with their keepers. In terms of intelligence, they're on par with a dog and can be taught to come when called or perform basic tricks.

Though un-neutered males may have a faint fruity, musky aroma, most sugar gliders have no noticeable odor. Their grooming needs are minimal—they don't require regular baths, and though you may need to trim their nails about once a month, you can also provide cage furnishings that keep their nails short naturally. Given a healthy diet and suitable environment, sugar gliders are hardy animals and aren't prone to health problems. Finding a vet can be tricky since they are rarer pets, but they don't rack up the costly vet bills common in some exotic mammals.

In terms of human health concerns, sugar gliders have been known to trigger some pet allergies. The area around their cages will require daily cleaning to prevent the build-up of bacteria and mold—sugar gliders aren't the cleanest animals, and they'll frequently throw waste or food through the bars of their cage. Gliders also have a powerful set of teeth and will use them for defense if they feel threatened.

Sugar glider bites are painful and on rare occasions can be deep enough to require stitches. Well-socialized sugar gliders rarely bite, but a keeper should expect to get nipped at least once in the course of a 10-year lifespan.

Legality

In North America, sugar gliders are considered wild or exotic pets, meaning their potential threat to the habitats and life cycles of native species if released are unknown. There are no federal restrictions on sugar glider ownership in the US or Canada, but there may be on the state and local level. As of the writing of this book, sugar gliders are illegal as pets in Alaska, California, Georgia, Hawaii, Massachusetts, and New Mexico. They're also restricted in select areas of Minnesota, Utah, Ontario, and British Columbia. Some states, like Pennsylvania, require you to obtain a permit before purchasing sugar gliders. Make sure to check with your local Fish & Wildlife Office to determine what steps you have to take to legally own your animal before buying one. If discovered, animals that are kept illegally are removed from their owner's home and either sent to a rescue organization or—more often—euthanized.

Cost of sugar glider ownership

The initial costs of sugar glider ownership are high. For a single standard-colored joey, you should expect to pay anywhere from $150 to $300. More unique colorations can cost upwards of $2000, depending on the individual and breeder. Since you shouldn't keep a single sugar glider, the cost of the animals alone is often in the thousands. Sugar gliders do occasionally show up at animal rescue organizations, and you can find listings online of animals in need of a new home, often for free or at least a whole lot cheaper than you'd find them from a breeder. You can also find adult sugar gliders that are retired breeding animals for less money. These animals may take longer to bond with since you're not the first owner, but can often make equally loving, wonderful pets if you've got more time than money.

The cost of the cage and its furnishings for sugar gliders is also high. Since they need so much space, you should budget around $200-$300 for the enclosure and necessary supplies, including a high-quality running wheel, food and water dishes, sleeping pouches, and plenty of toys to keep your gliders occupied.

It's a good idea to take your new pets to the vet for a check-up as soon as you bring them home. A typical exam visit for a sugar glider runs around $50-$100. If you buy a male animal, you'll most likely want to get him neutered. This procedure typically costs in the range of $100-$350, depending on your vet. Since they're not prone to many illnesses, sugar gliders don't require any vaccinations or shots.

Once you have them at home, the ongoing costs of sugar glider ownership are about on par with those of a cat. Most of their food will be the same things you eat yourself—low-fat meats and fresh fruits and vegetables. The pre-packaged insectivore chow that they should get as a portion of their diet is a bit more expensive than a bag of cat or dog food—about $8-$10 a pound—but they're small critters and only eat about ½ a tablespoon each per day. You can get crickets from the pet store for a couple dollars a dozen, and you can get a hundred mealworms for less than five bucks. Litters and beddings can cost between $10 and $30 a bag, but you can also use re-usable cage liners, with paper towels or newspaper underneath. While it's a good idea to start a vet fund in case of emergencies, sugar gliders are all told fairly inexpensive pets after the initial high investment.

Sugar gliders and children

Because of their daily and intricate care needs, sugar gliders are not good pets for young children. They need to be handled delicately during early bonding. Toddlers don't have the manual dexterity to hold a sugar glider correctly and it's usually best to have a "look don't touch" policy until the child reaches school age. Once they're old enough to understand how to hold and play with the pet correctly, you can allow supervised interaction. Make sure the children wash their hands thoroughly after handling the gliders, and keep an eye out for defensive behaviors. Take the glider back if it starts crabbing to avoid biting incidents. Older children and teens can help with sugar glider care, but remember what was said earlier about the animal's long lifespan. If you buy a sugar glider for a 15-year-old, you'll need to be ready to take over its care full-time once college starts.

Sugar gliders and other pets

The extent to which sugar gliders can co-exist with other animals inside the home is largely dependent on the personality of your other pets. Sugar gliders have been known to form close bonds with dogs and cats, considering them as much a part of the colony as their humans. There have also been reports of cats stalking and terrifying pet sugar gliders every time they're in the room together. Households with more docile dogs will be better environments for sugar gliders than those with yippy and excitable breeds, generally speaking. If you have large pets at home, look for the most outgoing sugar gliders you can find when you go to the breeder.

Because they're so scent-driven and can be territorial, sugar gliders are generally not known to get along well with ferrets—though again, there are exceptions. Birds and other small animals tend to co-exist with gliders peacefully, even sharing play time. Make sure you form a trust bond with your sugar glider first before making formal introductions to the other animals in the home.

Chapter 2: Housing and Supplies

Though they're small creatures, a sugar glider's activity level—combined with the fact that it's best to keep them in groups—means you need to have a fairly large enclosure to keep your glider healthy. Remember that sugar gliders are arboreal (tree-dwelling) critters. They do best in a cage with a lot of vertical space, and hanging toys, ledges, or pieces of fleece that they can hang, climb, and snuggle on are necessary components of an ideal sugar glider environment. A high-quality exercise wheel and durable food and water containers are also necessary to the glider's long-term health.

Because they're still largely considered an exotic animal, there's no "sugar glider" section in most major pet stores, and you might have trouble finding everything you need at a brick and mortar store. Larger breeders often offer cages, toys, and pouches for sale, either in their shops or online; other keepers choose to make their glider's cage or furnishings. In any case, gathering all the supplies may be more difficult than it would be for a more common pet, and you should secure everything you need before you buy your animal, just in case things prove more difficult to find than you anticipated.

The Cage

Minimum dimensions for a sugar glider enclosure are about 32" by 20", with a height of 3 feet or more. Bigger is better, and you should buy the largest cage you can. Taller and narrower is generally better than shorter and wider, but the exact dimensions can vary. Keep in mind that you need to be able to clean the cage effectively. Wider cages may also have difficulty fitting through doorways, so make sure to measure your space carefully and decide whether that will be an issue.

Metal bars are the best material for a sugar glider cage. Make sure the bars are no more than ½" apart so you don't have any escapees, and that any materials or paints used to coat them are non-toxic. Don't use any solid construction materials that have a smooth surface, like glass, plastic, or varnished wood. Sugar gliders can't climb or grip these surfaces, and animals kept in cages of these materials tend to develop painful hip and joint problems. These materials also don't provide very good ventilation, and at least two walls of the cage should be open metal bars, with any solid sides covered in bark, fleece, or some other material that the sugar gliders can hang on to.

Tower cages

Made for keeping ferrets, sugar gliders, and other arboreal mammals, these cages are easy to find online and are generally less expensive to purchase on the internet than through large pet stores, for whom they're more of a specialty item (if they carry them at all). What's nice about these cages is they often come with platforms and ramps that can be arranged within the cage to make the perfect glider environment. They also often have multiple doors, making it easier both to clean the cage and to interact with your animals. These cages are some of the best value options, typically running in the $100 to $200 range.

Large bird cages

The bird section of your pet store can be your best source for sugar glider cages. Since they're made for flying animals, they've got a good height to width ratio, and bird cages often come with a wheeled stand for easy movement and an under-cage litter pan design that can be very helpful in keeping the enclosure clean. Hexagonal, corner, and rectangular cages can all be good options, though the corner models may be more difficult to clean. Depending on the size and design, these cages can cost anywhere from $100 to $500.

Modular cage designs

If the large size of the tower and bird cage designs is too unwieldy for your space, a modular design consisting of two or more cages might do the trick. You can remove the shared walls and tie the cages together to give your gliders a large space to glide through. When it's time to move or clean the cages, you can reattach the missing walls and move the gliders into one cage or the other. Though more expensive to set up as each cage is likely to cost around $100 to $200, these modular designs can be especially useful for managing a larger colony or a breeding population.

Cage placement

Given the immense size of the enclosure, where you put your sugar glider cage in your home is going to depend largely on where it fits. Most people will put them in a living room, family room, or den. Even if your bedroom is large enough for the cage, it's not recommended unless you're an incredibly heavy sleeper. There is no such thing as a truly silent exercise wheel, and your sugar gliders will make a decent amount of noise in their nightly foraging and play.

Aside from space and noise concerns, the main thing you should keep in mind when positioning your glider cage within the home is to avoid any excessively hot or cold spots. Sugar gliders are accustomed to high heat and have fur to protect them from the cold, but too many variations in temperature too frequently can still make them sick. Avoid areas in front of windows, directly under heating and air-conditioning vents, or too close to doorways—all of these places have a tendency to create temperature fluctuations and drafts. Windows can be especially dangerous, since the sunlight coming through the glass can create a greenhouse effect and overheat your gliders.

Temperature and humidity requirements

The ideal temperature range for sugar gliders is between 72°F and 80°F, with a relative humidity of 50%. Unlike desert animals, sugar gliders don't typically need supplemental heat, and don't require an enclosure that's heated to tropical temperatures. Sugar gliders occasionally do experience cold winter weather and even snow in the wild, and survive by cuddling together and sharing warmth as a colony.

Your sugar gliders will do the same thing in captivity, and aside from perhaps providing thicker sleeping pouches in the winter months, you shouldn't have to use any supplemental heating for your main sugar glider cage, provided it's kept in a room with an ambient temperature above 50°F. If the room is comfortable for human habitation, it should be equally comfortable for your "suggies".

If you live in an area that gets cold during the winter, you may want to obtain some kind of supplemental heat source for your secondary cage, especially if your glider needs medical attention during the cooler months. If you are using an extra heat source, don't use any kind of heat lamp or ceramic heat emitter. These will make the metal bars too warm, causing burns to your sugar gliders when they make contact. Similarly, hot rocks or heat rocks designed for reptile use are unsuitable for sugar gliders. These devices are heating coils covered in resin, which can thin and create hot spots likely to burn your glider. Direct contact with the heating rocks can also heat the sugar gliders too much, causing heat stroke or dehydration.

A simple 4 or 8 watt heating pad is often the best option to provide extra heat to a sugar glider enclosure. Never put the heating pad directly in the cage—your suggies may burn themselves on it, or chew through the wire and electrocute themselves. It's better to put it along the side of the cage, close to the nest box or sleeping pouch. You can also make or buy a nestbox with a small separate compartment for the heating pad. In either of these cases, make sure to set up an external probe in the area where the sugar gliders will be, and link it to a thermostat to automatically shut off the heating pad once it reaches 70°F. It can be just as dangerous for your pets to get too hot as it is for them to get too cold.

Not much research has been done into the proper photoperiod maintenance of sugar gliders in captivity. If you're not familiar with the term, an animal's photoperiod simply refers to how much light it's accustomed to receiving during a normal day. While it's a term most commonly associated with keeping reptiles, it's also important for the long-term health of other small mammals, especially warm-weather nocturnal species. Since they don't require supplemental heat, it is not the current practice to set up a timed lighting system for sugar glider enclosures, but a home with electric lights doesn't accurately simulate the natural day and night patterns your gliders experience in the wild, and some individuals will be more sensitive to this fact than others. If you notice signs of stress in your gliders and can't figure out the cause, consider a bright light near the cage on a 12-hour timer. It can be a regular incandescent bulb—it's not for heat or basking, like it would be for a reptile—but the consistent shift of light levels will help regulate your animal's metabolic rhythm. If the glider enclosure is in a room with lots of light even at night, a screen or curtain that can be pulled across the area with the glider's cage can also help ease the light pollution that's throwing off his mental clock.

Flooring

A lot of bird cages are equipped with a wire floor and a tray or litter pan underneath to catch the droppings. This is a great construction for a sugar glider cage, as well, because it keeps the gliders from walking through their own waste, but the open wire can be difficult for the gliders to walk on and you should cover it with something soft. Fleece cage liners can be great for this. Since fleece is hydrophobic (holding less than 1% of its weight in water) any urine or spilled water will flow straight through into the litter pan beneath, leaving no wet spots and limiting bacterial growth. You'll need to change the liners often, no less frequently than every other day, so keep at least two on hand. Many keepers find it useful to keep sets of 6-8, laundering the liners in a single load once a week.

If the floor is solid, a cage liner of some kind is still a good idea to help keep the cage clean. If you use a fleece liner, put a piece of newspaper or paper towel underneath the liner to absorb any liquid that comes through it. Synthetic cage liners from the small animal or reptile section can also work well, though they're more absorbent than fleece and will need to be changed daily. Newsprint and butcher paper can also serve well, but they will need to be removed and disposed of daily.

Spot-cleanable litter options

You shouldn't use clay or clumpable kitty litter in a sugar glider enclosure, even if it has a removable tray and your pets won't be walking through the litter. The dust produced by these types of litters can irritate the respiratory tract of the animals and can lead to infections and breathing problems. You should also avoid any litters or beddings made of pine or cedar. The aromatic hydrocarbons (also called phenols) that make these woods smell so pleasant can be very damaging to the lungs and respiratory tract of small mammals. The toxins can also cause liver damage and even organ failure from prolonged exposure.

When using scoopable litters, you should spot-clean them daily with a litter scoop or designated slotted spoon, and replace the entire litter no less often than once a week. Yesterday's news and other pelleted recycled paper litters are the favorite of many sugar glider keepers. These litters are highly absorbent and free of both odor and dust. Softer recycled paper beddings also work great as sugar glider litters, and have the advantage over pelleted forms of being lighter in color, making it easier to locate soiled areas. Recycled paper bedding is also softer, and can be especially useful in a cage with no litter pan. The disadvantage of both pelleted and fluffier recycled paper options is the cost. Pelleted litters run about $10 for a 13 pound bag; recycled paper beddings run between $20 and $30 for a 25 liter bag. Most keepers find that re-usable liners, though a bigger initial investment, are cheaper in the long-term.

Secondary enclosures

Due to the large size of sugar glider cages, you'll probably find it helpful to have a smaller, secondary cage on-hand to use for transportation to vet visits, or to quarantine sick or injured animals. As with the main cage, this secondary cage should be taller than it is wide, though you should also make sure it'll fit comfortably in your car, and that it's easy for you to pick up and move.

Exercise wheel

Even given a lot of space to glide and play, sugar gliders should be provided with an exercise wheel to help them stay active during their in-cage time. Avoid traditional hamster wheel designs with open mesh running tracks—sugar glider toes and limbs can get stuck in the little holes, often causing injury. The support structure of these wheels is also dangerous for sugar gliders, whose bushy tails can get pinched or caught while they're running. Avoid any wheel that has a center axle—side-mounted designs tend to work best. In terms of size, you want to look for a wheel that's 9" to 12" in diameter.

Stealth wheels are popular among many small animal owners. There's no such thing as a truly silent wheel, but stealth wheels come closer than any other model, especially great for nocturnal species. Though they may initially look like the running track has the same bad design as the hamster wheel, it's actually a larger mesh of plastic, and doesn't present the same toe-catching risks. Other similar designs, like Velociraptor wheels, are also excellent options.

Sugar gliders seem to love "Wodent Wheels". Most gliders will find the Senior model more comfortable, although especially small animals may feel more at ease on the Junior size, and especially large gliders might not want to use this design, since the front panel may restrict their natural running movements. There're no dangerous pinch points on the frame, and the front cover with the small holes cut out is especially appealing to gliders, who love climbing into holes and cubbies and will be especially drawn to the gaps on the front of the Wodent Wheel.

If you want to avoid having to trim your glider's nails as often, you can buy modified wheels with a soft sand abrasive running track insert. Put the track into the wheel for a day or two each month and your sugar glider will file his nails down as he runs. You can also buy the trimming track separately and sized to fit a variety of popular wheel brands and sizes.

Food dishes

Hanging food dishes are best for sugar gliders because they work with their natural instincts. Sugar gliders are used to eating in and off of trees, so they like to be fed up high. You can put a platform, hanging rope, or branch under or near the dishes to give the gliders more space to eat. Stainless steel is the best material for food dishes because it's easy to clean and extremely durable—remember that your sugar gliders will be gliding to them, standing on them, and probably trying to play with them. Ceramic dishes can also be suitable, provided you have a sturdy enough device to hold them. You want to make sure to get food dishes that won't break and can be firmly secured to the side of the cage. The size of bowls you need is largely dependent on how many animals you have sharing the enclosure. For two sugar gliders, you'll only need to put about a tablespoon of food in each daily, so the main concern is that they're wide enough at the top for the gliders to gain access. Larger colonies will need larger dishes, or more dishes scattered around the enclosure. Each set of dishes should consist of at least two pieces: One dish for the staple food that's left in the cage throughout the day, and another for the protein and veggies that you offer in the evening and then remove. It's a good idea to have two sets of dishes so one can be in the cage while you're washing the other.

Water bottles

It's generally better to use a bottle than a dish to provide water for your suggies. Sugar gliders are extremely active and fairly messy. A water dish is likely to be knocked over, stepped in, or used as a bathroom as much as it's used for drinking. This could create unsanitary conditions in the water, making it more likely for your gliders to get sick, or could mean they're without water for extended periods until you notice they've kicked over their dish again. With water bottles, you'll be able to accurately track how much water your gliders are drinking, and know it's always available and clean.

Plastic water bottles can give their contents an odd taste that will prevent some sugar gliders from drinking, and though they might work with your animal, most breeders recommend using glass water bottles with sugar gliders. Glass bottles are more durable and aren't much more expensive, usually costing $5 to $10 each, though you'll likely have a better chance of finding them online than in your local pet store.

Food storage and preparation

Most of the food you give your sugar glider will come from the grocery store—the same fruits, veggies, and meats you eat yourself. The notable exception to this that you should consider before bringing your glider home are the insects that are a necessary component of any healthy and varied sugar glider diet. Mealworms can be kept for extended periods of time in the plastic container they're sold in. The sawdust-like material in the container with them serves as both food and shelter, and they'll do fine left to their own devices either at room temperature or chilled in the refrigerator. Crickets, grasshoppers, and other beetles, on the other hand, will need some kind of living quarters inside your home. Even if you only buy a few insects at a time, you have to be able to keep them long enough to gut-load them (a process of increasing the nutritional value of insect food that's discussed in more detail in chapter 4). They don't need much space, though you should make sure the walls are smooth and tall enough the crickets can't escape when you open the container to feed or retrieve them. A simple 5.5-gallon plastic or glass terrarium will serve nicely, or even a plastic storage container of suitable dimensions with a tight-sealing lid and holes cut near the top for ventilation.

Sleeping and snuggling

In the wild, sugar glider colonies live in the hollows of trees, and they feel most comfortable sleeping in tight spaces, curled up with their family. You want to offer your gliders a variety of sleeping area options—a good rule of thumb is one or two per animal. These generally take two main forms: sleeping pouches or nesting boxes.

Sleeping pouches, also called snuggle bags, are cloth bags made of fleece or some other soft and insulated fabric. Usually around 6" to 12" on a side, these bags are designed to hang from the side of the cage to provide a safe, warm, and natural place for your gliders to rest. You can either buy them online for $5 to $10 each or—if you're the crafty type—make your own with lined fleece from the craft store (you can find free patterns on most sugar glider forums). Similar products, like hammocks and pouches made for ferrets and other small animals, can also work well as hangout or nesting spots. Just make sure they're well made, with no fraying threads that can catch a tone or snout, and that they're made with a hydrophobic material like fleece.

Nesting boxes are another sleeping option for your sugar gliders. Some breeders prefer nesting boxes over sleeping pouches because they find it easier to check on the parents and the new joeys without disturbing the nest. Plastic or acrylic nesting boxes are generally better than wood models because they're easier to clean and don't retain moisture or odors. You can find great nesting boxes in both the small animal and bird sections of the pet store. If you use a nesting box, you'll want to put some kind of soft material inside for the gliders to cuddle up with. If you're using recycled paper bedding that will work nicely, or scraps of fleece or flannel (just make sure to check the edges for fraying threads).

Bonding pouch

A bonding pouch is like a mobile sleeping pouch that lets you take your glider with you without worrying about his security. They're a great tool in the initial bonding process since it lets the new pet get accustomed to your smell and voice without requiring direct contact. They're often made of fleece, similar to sleeping pouches, but rather than having an open top, the upper flap can be zipped securely closed, with an open mesh window on the front to keep the air fresh and let your glider see the world. You can find a wide array of styles and colors available online, and they cost about $10 to $20 each.

Other cage furnishings

Sugar gliders are active and curious by nature, and the more engaging you can make their enclosure, the happier your animals will be. The most successful toys will work with their natural behaviors—gliding, nesting, foraging, and exploring. Puzzle toys with treats inside (from the bird or small animal sections) tend to be especially popular with gliders. Since they're not rodents and don't need to file their teeth down, wood toys designed for chewing made for other small animals are not ideal—they won't necessarily be harmful to a glider, but he won't enjoy it as much as a hamster would. The best toys for gliders are the ones that encourage climbing and exploring.

You should also provide your gliders with plenty of landing and lounging areas. Hanging ropes or plastic link chains sold for birds are often good, as are ledges, branches, and perches. You can buy these items at the pet store, but you can also use kids' toys, shelving from the home improvement store, or even branches from the trees in your backyard, if they're the right size and sturdy. Any item being introduced to the enclosure second-hand or from the outside should be disinfected with a 10% bleach solution, rinsed until the smell of the bleach is gone, then allowed to dry completely before going in the cage, just to make sure it's not carrying any nasty micro-organisms. Just like

with the cage and bedding, make sure you're not

using anything containing cedar or pine and that all

paints used in the products are non-toxic and lead-

free.

Chapter 3: Buying your gliders (and bringing them home)

You've decided you're ready for sugar glider ownership, you've determined they're legal in your area, and you've set up a beautiful cage that's just waiting for your pets to fill it. So where do you find your pets—and how do you know which ones to buy?

The most important thing is to purchase healthy animals. A healthy sugar glider has sleek and shiny unbroken fur. Un-neutered sexually mature males will have a bald spot on their foreheads, but otherwise there should be no interruptions to the smooth coat. Look very carefully at the glider's face. The ears should be perky and upright, and the eyes should be wide and bright, with no discharge coming from the eyes, ears, or nose. Unneutered males may give off a faintly fruity, musky aroma, but there should otherwise be no noticeable odor. Finally, watch the way the sugar glider runs around his cage and interacts with his surroundings. He should be fairly active and alert, and should have a smooth, easy gait, with no dragging limbs. It's natural if the gliders don't warm to you at first—they're naturally wary of new smells—but they should be responsive to handling by the people they're familiar with. If the sugar gliders start to crab or take on a defensive posture with their breeder, that's a bad sign. At the very least, the animal will be more of a challenge to bond with, and he may also have been mistreated or neglected, which could make it difficult to build trust.

Unless you're adding on to an existing colony, you shouldn't plan on buying a single sugar glider. They're accustomed to living in family groups and aren't psychologically equipped to a solitary life. While sugar gliders bond readily with their human keepers, no amount of human interaction can replace the companionship of their own kind. Kept alone, sugar gliders will get depressed, lethargic, withdrawn, and defensive. They'll often self-mutilate, refuse food, and get physically ill—to put it poetically, solitary sugar gliders can actually die of loneliness.

Setting up a colony

If you're a new sugar glider owner, it's best to start with a pair of animals. They can keep each other company, but their care won't overwhelm you and you'll be able to give both animals the attention they deserve. If you can find siblings that's even better, since the animals will know each other and will already have a bond. It's also best to start out with a pair of animals that can't breed so you can get the hang of caring for adult sugar gliders before you have to concern yourself with raising and caring for joeys. Though it's not healthy for females to breed until they're about two years old, they're capable of reproducing as early as nine months out of pouch. Animals kept in the same cage that are capable of breeding will breed whether you want them to or not. Accidental pregnancies are stressful for both you and your pet, and it'll be best for everyone to avoid the situation entirely.

Two female sugar gliders are probably the easiest to start with. Two male sugar gliders can often get along fine on their own with no females around, though if females are introduced they may fight for dominance, and are more likely to show aggressive or territorial behavior. If you want to keep both genders in the same enclosure without the risk of breeding, you can get the males neutered. Sugar gliders can be neutered as young as four months out of pouch, and should be neutered before any females in the enclosure reach nine months of age. Since they're marsupials, it's pretty easy to tell the males from the females—females will be the ones with pouches on their bellies, which will look like an inch-wide slit on their bellies when there aren't any joeys inside.

What age to buy

Most breeders recommend buying sugar gliders when they're around 8 to 10 months out of pouch. In the wild, this is when most joeys will leave home to find a group of other joeys their own age and form a new colony. Instinctually, they're looking to form new bonds at this stage of their life, and will quickly accept you as part of the family. It's also possible to form loving, long-term bonds with full-grown sugar gliders, but it usually takes a bit longer for the animals to get used to your presence.

If you're buying a companion or mate for an adult sugar glider, it's recommended to buy an adult around your pet's age. This is especially important with a mate to encourage healthy breeding. Even if you're not breeding, it can be dangerous to introduce joeys into the established enclosures of adults, especially those of un-neutered males. The colony's alpha male will have an instinctual desire to defend his territory, and while he'll eventually accept the newcomer as part of the colony, these initial displays can injure or kill a joey. Alternatively, if you think you can adequately care for two new animals, you could buy a pair of joeys around the same age and keep them in a separate enclosure near the main one so the animals can get to know each others' scents. The joeys can keep each other company until they're accepted into the established colony or they're big enough to hold their own.

Coat options

Thanks to the wonders of selective breeding, you can find sugar gliders in a variety of stunning colorations—if you're willing to pay for it. While animals with standard colorations typically cost around $200-$300 per animal, more unique colorations can run into the thousands.

If the sugar glider has basically the same coloration as a standard but darker, with more defined markings, they're known as a black beauty. If it's mostly light silver in color but still has darker markings on its back and face, it's known as a platinum. Leucistic sugar gliders have cream-colored fur and black eyes; there are also true albinos, with white fur and red eyes, and cremeino animals, who have cream-colored fur and red eyes. Finally, some sugar gliders are bred to have distinctive patterning on their bodies. Mosaic patterns have the standard white and gray colors but in different arrangements than in standard sugar gliders. Piebald patterns, a variation on the mosaic, are mostly white with patches of darker color, typically on the sides.

Coat color variations are superficial only, and have no effect on the health of the animal. There is a misconception that albino animals have shorter lifespans. This is true in the wild, where their lack of pigment makes them stand out and puts them at a greater risk of predation, but in captivity they have no more health issues than their standard-colored counterparts. If you're interested in buying a specific color pattern, you may need to look for your sugar glider online and have it shipped from a breeder. This can be costly—around $200-$300—but is safe for the animals if they're bought from an established breeder with experience shipping pets.

Where to get your sugar glider

Since they're exotic pets, finding a sugar glider is not typically as easy as finding a hamster or a guinea pig. Captive breeding programs have expanded across

North America, and if you live in a major metropolitan area you probably won't have to go far to find an animal. If you're in a more rural area, you may be looking at a long drive to visit a breeder, or else having the animals shipped to you.

As they've gained popularity sugar gliders have started showing up for sale occasionally at mall kiosks and fair booths. Be especially wary of animals you see for sale in these settings. If the animals are kept in suitably-sized cages and look happy and healthy, talk to the person selling them and gauge how much they know about the animals. It may be a breeder selling her pets in a new setting, but most of these sellers won't be able to sell you healthy pets. Whether through ignorance or to increase their yield, disreputable breeders will often keep unneutered males in the same enclosure with their daughters or siblings, resulting in inbreeding that can give their offspring both health and behavioral problems.

It is always best with a new pet to see and interact with the animal before buying it, but as mentioned above, in some areas of the world that just might not be possible. If you have to go through an online distributor, be very thorough in your research. Breeders that sell products related to sugar gliders are fine; breeders that want to sell you information about taking care of sugar gliders are typically disreputable. Be mindful of the tone of the breeder's website. Does it sound to you like they care about the animals, or like they're trying to sell them to you? If they care more about the money than the animals, you may end up with a sick or unsocialized pet. Avoid any breeder that recommends keeping solitary sugar gliders or suggests they can survive on pelleted foods alone. These are human-centric rather than animal-centric breeders. Finally, be wary of organizations that call their animals "sugar bears" instead of "sugar gliders."

The majority of these are part of a national franchise known for mistreatment of their animals.

Buying from breeders

The best option is to visit a nearby breeder to buy your sugar gliders. Shopping straight from a breeder means you can ask a lot of questions about this specific animal's care, lineage, and personality that a second-hand seller might not know. Breeders may also be able to give you information about where to find a good exotic pet veterinarian, and frequently provide post-adoption support if any health problems or issues should arise. Checking out your animals in person also lets you find pets that are perfectly suited to you. Think of the pet buying process as a two-way interview. You're about to start a long relationship with these animals, and you want to find pets that seem open to you and that you yourself are drawn to.

The website Sugar Glider Help (http://www.sugargliderhelp.com/) features a list of breeders broken down by state. In most areas, you'll be able to find a breeder within a couple hours of where you live. If you go in to the state listings, you can also see reviews and ratings of the breeders to help you decide if they're someone you want to contact.

Exotic pet stores

If there's a pet store in your area that specializes in exotic mammals, they're likely to sell sugar gliders—or at least know where to get them if you ask. Exotic pet stores are often more discerning in where they get their animals and tend to know more about the animals they sell than the employees of national chains. Though an exotic pet should be able to tell you the name of the breeder where their animals were raised, they will likely not have the same information about the animal's family history, if that's information you'd want to know. Post-adoption support is generally not as strong as buying from a breeder, and you'll likely have fewer animals to choose from than with a larger breeder.

Animal rescue organizations

While you may not find sugar gliders at your local humane society, there are sugar glider rescue organizations throughout North America, and these organizations have grown in the past few years. It's the unfortunate reality that as the popularity of a pet species increases, so too does the rate of animals that get abandoned due to owners losing interest or being overwhelmed. Rescued sugar gliders can be more time-consuming pets. The cumulative effects of neglect and abuse can make them more wary of humans, and you may have to spend a long time rebuilding the animal's trust. Past issues with their diet and environment can also lead to health problems that could cause higher vet bills down the line. Rescued sugar gliders may not be the best pets for first-time owners—after all, you're doing the animals no favors if you can't handle the advanced care and end up abandoning them again. If you feel up to the challenge, however, rescued pets can make sweet and loving additions to the family, and they come with the added benefit of knowing you've saved an animal's life. The other advantage of rescued pets is that they're significantly cheaper than buying joeys first-hand from a breeder.

SunCoast Sugar Gliders offers an online sugar glider exchange forum (http://www.sugar-gliders.com/glider-exchange.htm) where owners can sell animals that need new homes. Unlike the abandoned pets found at rescue organizations, these sugar gliders often come from loving homes that have to give their pets up due to a sudden life change.

Though these pets will typically be adults and may take a bit longer to get used to you than a joey, they won't come with the health issues associated with rescues. They're also typically cheaper than joeys from breeders (sometimes they're even free to a good home) and may come with cages, toys, and other care supplies, making your job easier and your glider's transition smoother. If there're no animals listed on the exchange near you, listing sites like Craigslist or Hoobly may also be places to find good pets looking for a loving home.

Bringing your pets home

When you first bring your glider home, it's a good idea to give it a day or two to adjust to its new surroundings before starting the bonding process. Give them food and water and keep an eye on the cage to make sure they're settling in. If one of your new gliders wants to check you out while you're doing this there's no reason to deny them, but if they'd rather watch you from a distance for a couple days that's okay, too. If you want to help the bonding process along, you can put their sleeping pouch or other cloth furnishings under your pillow for a few nights before you bring the animals home; this will start instantly associating your smell with comfort. You could also put an old t-shirt in the enclosure to serve the same purpose.

Sugar gliders are very intelligent animals and their personalities vary widely from animal to animal. In these first couple of days, pay close attention to how they interact with each other and their environment. Don't be alarmed or concerned if a new glider takes a defensive posture or starts crabbing when you approach the cage. It's natural for them to be wary of their new circumstances, and the behavior should stop once they get to know you.

Shortly after bringing home your animals, it's a good idea to set them up a vet visit. Do this after they've had a bit of time to adjust and you've started the bonding process—say around 1-2 weeks after you buy them. This is a chance to make sure they're starting with a clean bill of health. It also introduces you to your closest vet—and your vet to your animals—so that you don't have to scramble if something goes wrong in the future. Finally, the vet can answer any questions that have come up since bringing your animal home.

Bonding with your sugar glider

After it's had a couple of days to settle, the most important ingredient to forming a tight, trusting bond is to spend as much time as possible around your animal—at least an hour with each animal each day. Most keepers find it easiest to start the bonding process during the daytime, when the glider is still a bit groggy and not likely to be as feisty and active. Bond with each new animal individually. Start by putting a single joey into a bonding pouch and carrying him around with you. If he seems agitated, talk to him softly and calmly, and don't try to touch him until he's calmed down. If he falls asleep while he's in the pouch, this is a good sign; it means he feels safe and calm with you nearby.

When it seems like the sugar glider is calm in his bonding pouch with you, try opening the pouch and slowly putting your hand into the bag to pet him. If the animal starts crabbing or pulls back into a defensive posture, stop moving your hand forward but don't instantly withdraw it. You need to teach the pet that you're not a threat, and the only way to do that is fighting through the defensive behavior. If a minute or two passes and the glider shows no signs of relaxing— or if the animal bites you—then you can try stroking it from the outside of the bonding pouch instead. Keep some mealworms or diced fruit on hand as treats and give them to your glider throughout the bonding process. Remember that the goal is to give the animal positive associations with your smell, so don't get frustrated or yell at the animal even if it does bite. This will only serve to make them more wary of you in the future.

Bonding with a new sugar glider can take anywhere from a few days to a few months, depending on the animal. Even if they come from the same litter, no two gliders are exactly the same. Your most important tool as you're bonding with your animal is patience. Listen to your animal's behaviors and do what you can to make him feel safe, and you'll be rewarded in kind with your animal's trust.

Introductions to other animals

Separate enclosures are a big help in introducing new joeys to adults. Set up the cages side by side, or as close as you're able to get them. You'll likely notice the gliders chirping and sniffing at each other across the distance. Just like with bonding to humans, give the new gliders a couple days to adjust before trying an up close introduction. It's best to do the introductions in a neutral space—wherever you let them out to play should be fine. Supervise the introduction carefully and be ready to separate the animals if a fight breaks out. While the animals are out of their cages, consider swapping their sleeping pouches. This is similar to putting an old t-shirt in the cage—it gets them used to each others' scents and helps associate that smell with comfort. You'll find it's more difficult to introduce new animals of any age to an un-neutered adult male than to neutered males and females.

If you have other pets in your house, wait until the glider is completely comfortable and bonded with you before trying to introduce the sugar glider to them. Most dogs and even cats can bond with sugar gliders and learn not to hassle them, but it's very dependant on the personalities of your individual animals. A dog or cat can easily injure a small animal like a sugar glider, even if it's just trying to play and has no malicious intent. Keep the sugar glider secure in its bonding pouch during the first introduction. Curious sniffing and gentle pawing or nuzzling is fine; attempts to bite or claw are a sign you shouldn't let them share any playtime. Even if your larger pets seem to get along great with your sugar gliders, you should carefully supervise all interactions.

Chapter 4: Feeding and Care

A well-balanced diet is key to maintaining the long-term health of your sugar glider. Like with his toys and cage furnishings, when it comes to food, variety is key. Just like human beings need to eat a range of foods from different categories to get all the nutrients they need, a sugar glider isn't going to get all the vitamins and minerals it requires from any single source. For this reason, there is no pelleted or other commercial product on the market that is considered acceptable for full-time exclusive use.

In the wild, sugar gliders are primarily insectivores. During the months when insects are sparse, wild gliders will rip the bark from tree trunks with their teeth and suck out the sap. They'll also supplement their diet with nectar, eggs, small mammals, and birds. While a sugar glider's diet in the wild is mostly protein, even very active sugar gliders in captivity don't have to expend as much energy to forage and evade predators, and are less likely to experience injury. As such, the ideal balance in a captive sugar glider's diet is about 40% protein for non-breeding animals and 50% for breeding animals and pregnant females. The rest of the glider's diet should consist of a variety of fruits and vegetables, high in protein and low in fat and phosphorus, with supplements to round out the nutritional balance.

The ideal diet of a sugar glider can be best understood by breaking it down into four basic categories: Fruits and vegetables, proteins, staple food, and supplements. You'll occasionally come across a picky animal who will only select their favorite foods from whatever is offered. It's important to monitor your gliders during feeding time for this reason. Since you'll be keeping at least two individuals in any sugar glider enclosure, it can be difficult to tell who's eating what unless you watch them do it. If you've got new gliders that are being particularly picky eaters, it's a good idea to call the breeder where you got the animal and ask what kind of diet they use. Though they enjoy variety, sugar gliders can sometimes be thrown off by rapid or sweeping change. The combination of the new home and new food might just be too much for him right now, and offering him the familiar food he's used to will likely make him start eating again.

In general, major changes to a sugar glider's diet—even if they're positive and will improve their health—should be done gradually. This doesn't mean you have to worry if you had to buy pears instead of apples for his fruit this week, but if you're introducing, live insects to the diet of a glider previously fed on cooked chicken, or fresh fruits and veggies to a glider who'd before only eaten pelleted chow, you should be prepared for the transition to take a couple of weeks.

What to avoid

Before we get into the specifics of a sugar glider's diet, let's take a moment to discuss things that sugar gliders shouldn't eat. First of all, you want to avoid any product that contains a lot of artificial ingredients, whether they're preservatives or flavorings and colorings. A glider's smaller body is more susceptible to toxins than a larger human form, and these substances can accumulate in the animal's organs, leading to problems with the liver and kidneys. A specific mention is due to the compound Menadione, which is a nasty component of some supplements (largely used as an inexpensive livestock micro-nutrient) that has been linked to brain and liver disorders and should be avoided.

Since sugar gliders are omnivores, most commercial pet foods aren't suitable even as staple foods. Cats, dogs, and ferrets are carnivores—the chow designed for them will be too heavy on protein and too high in fat, often leading to obesity. Most small animal diets have the opposite issue. Made for animals that are primarily herbivores, they don't have enough animal protein, and the nuts and fruits have too much fat and sugar.

There are a few foods with a known toxicity to sugar gliders that should be avoided at all costs. Never let your sugar glider eat a lightning bug. The compounds that make it glow are also highly toxic and could be very harmful to all small pets. The same generally goes for any wild bugs in your area that are brightly-colored, like lady bugs, or have stingers or fangs, like spiders and wasps. In terms of vegetables, avoid feeding your sugar glider any aromatics—this includes onions, garlic, scallions, and other similar foods. The thiosulfate contained in these vegetables is highly toxic to most pets, causing a condition known as hemolytic anemia where the red blood cells are damaged, often fatally, within two weeks of consuming the offending vegetable. Also avoid rhubarb, which has levels of calcium oxalate that may be fatal for small animals.

Foods that aren't immediately toxic but should still be avoided include junk foods like chocolate, that are high in sugar and fat, and high carbohydrate foods like bread. You should also avoid foods that are high in phosphorus, like beef, corn, nuts, seeds, and cottage cheese. Phosphorus can inhibit the body's absorption of calcium, eventually leading to a condition known as Metabolic Bone Disease (MBD) that causes spontaneous fractures and weakening of the skeletal structure and may lead to paralysis or even death. Beef should be avoided anyway because of its high fat content, as should pork and other fatty meats.

Though they're not bad in small amounts, you should also limit your glider's consumption of foods that are high in oxalates. Oxalates are naturally-occurring compounds in many foods that bind with iron and calcium, preventing full absorption. Many foods that are high in oxalates are also very nutritionally dense, making them otherwise excellent glider chow, so while you should limit consumption of high-oxalate foods to one serving a week, they can still feature in your glider's diet. These foods include many greens (collards, kale, chard, and spinach) as well as other vegetables like beans, beets, and eggplant, citrus fruits (especially the rinds), berries, and other tart fruits, like kiwi and grapes.

Fruits and vegetables

Your sugar glider should get one serving of fruits or vegetables daily. To picture the amount that would comprise a full serving, imagine cutting an apple into 8 equal-sized wedges. One of those wedges will feed two gliders. For less dense fruits, like watermelon, increase the serving size slightly. It's best to give your glider his fruits or vegetables in the evening, when he'd normally be preparing to go out and forage. As said above, variety is key. The more different kinds of fruits and vegetables you give your glider, the better chance for his nutrition to stay balanced. Try to maintain at least a 4-day rotation of fruits and vegetables, with a preference toward food high in iron, potassium, calcium, and vitamins A, B2, and C.

Melons are some of the best fruits to include in your weekly rotation. This includes watermelon, honeydew, and cantaloupe. Apples and pears of all varieties are also much-loved suggie treats, as are tropical fruits, like kiwi, bananas, and mangoes. The nutritional density of berries makes them worth feeding to your sugar gliders despite their typically high oxalate content, provided you limit them to one serving a week. Blueberries have an especially good balance of vitamins and minerals for a sugar glider. Carrots, sweet potatoes, yams, snap peas, and green beans make great vegetable offerings. This is obviously not a full list—other than the toxic vegetables mentioned above, almost any fruit or vegetable can be fair game for your sugar glider. It's the mixture of high-quality foods more than any single item that will keep your pet healthy.

With all fruits and vegetables, fresh is best, frozen is acceptable on occasion, and canned is right out. The reason for this has to do with nutrition and additives. The fresh versions of foods are going to have the most densely packed nutrients. Frozen foods may be lacking since most commercially frozen food is blanched before freezing, leeching out some of the vitamins and minerals, but so long as nothing has been added to them, they're still safe occasional foods for your glider. Canned fruits, on the other hand, tend to be packaged in a sweet syrup that has enough added sugar to all but negate the nutritional value of the product for your pet. Canned vegetables, similarly, may be packaged in water that's high in salt and oil and is generally bad for your suggie's nutrition.

When feeding your gliders fruits and vegetables, you want to make sure you give them pieces they can actually eat. Peel any fruit you would peel yourself before eating, like bananas and citrus fruits, and cut the fruit into bite-sized pieces for easier consumption (and remember, we're talking about your glider's bite-size here, not yours).

Proteins

Like with the fruits and veggies above, you want to feed your sugar gliders one serving of protein per day, in the evening when your gliders are getting ready to start their day. Again, variety is key, and you should strive to maintain at least a 4-day rotation of items. This is where sugar glider care gets a bit creepy crawly: When we're talking about proteins, most of the time, we're talking about bugs. At least three days of each week should feature some kind of live protein in your sugar glider's diet. These insects can include common feeder insects, like mealworms and crickets, or more esoteric offerings, like grasshoppers, locusts, or other beetles. Serving sizes of live insects will depend on the insect. Feed one locust, one large grasshopper, or 3-5 crickets (or cricket-sized beetles). Mealworms vary greatly in terms of size; feed 10-12 small mealworms, 7-10 medium-sized mealworms, or 3-5 large mealworms per animal per meal.

As far as people-food proteins, you want to stick to lean animal proteins over alternative protein products that are soy, corn, or whey based. Soy is especially bad because it contains female hormones (phytoestrogens) that can negatively effect a sugar glider's reproductive health. Cooked, unseasoned chicken can be a great protein, or a peeled boiled egg mixed with high protein cereal like corn flakes or Special K. Fruit-flavored yogurts can also be great. Pick a full-fat yogurt with no aspartame or other artificial sweeteners. Serving sizes for all human-edible proteins is one tablespoon for each pair of gliders per meal.

Keeping live food

If you've owned an insectivore before, you're likely familiar with the term gut-loading. This is a process by which crickets, mealworms, and other feeder insects are fed a diet of concentrated, highly nutritious food so that they're better for your pet. Commercial gut loads are available in the reptile section of the pet store. You should plan on buying your feeder insects far enough in advance that you can gut-load them for at least 24 hours before they're fed to your pets.

Mealworms are the exception to this rule, as they're typically sold in a gut-loaded sawdust material. Mealworms are by far the easiest feeder animal to keep. They require very little maintenance—throw a fresh slice of apple in their container for moisture every day and they'll be good to go. In fact, it's fairly easy to set up a self-sustaining mealworm colony. Simply move them to a plastic storage container that's at least six inches deep and fill it halfway with a mixture of oatmeal, whole-grain flour, and wheat bran (with apple slices for moisture). Make sure there're some holes poked in the lid for ventilation. The mealworm you feed to your sugar glider is actually the larval stage of the mealworm beetle. If left at room temperature, the mealworms will eventually pupate into their adult form. These beetles can also be fed to your sugar gliders, if you'd like, or left in the container to lay eggs and start your next generation of mealworms. Aside from replacing the apple slices daily and the flour mixture every few months, you won't have to do a thing until it's feeding time for your suggies. If you'd rather not deal with beetles, you can keep most mealworms in the refrigerator to halt their maturation process. Just don't do this with superworms or giant mealworms; those are tropical species and will die from hypothermia in the chilly air of your fridge.

A cricket enclosure requires a small amount more set-up than mealworms, though hardly any more maintenance. Some companies sell specifically designed cricket cages, typically acrylic terrariums with tube inserts in the side meant to make it easier to retrieve the insects at feeding time. These enclosures are generally overpriced, ineffective, and unnecessary. Though crickets are significantly more likely to escape their enclosure, a simple glass or acrylic terrarium will do that just as well, so long as you make sure the lid is secure and the walls are too slick to climb and too high to jump. Put a few empty toilet paper rolls or pieces of egg crate in the enclosure for the crickets to hide in. You can get a small plastic dish to feed them the gut load in, or simply sprinkle a bit over the bottom of the enclosure each morning. The trickiest thing about keeping crickets is giving them water. Crickets have a difficult time drinking from water dishes, and they're fairly likely to drown in the attempt. Just like with the mealworms, a piece of juicy fruit or vegetable in the cage should give them enough water. Apples, pears, and cucumbers all work great for this. Replace the fruit daily to prevent it from rotting or creating nasty bacteria your gliders shouldn't be eating. While it's not necessary to clean the cricket cage every day like you do with your glider enclosure, you should give it a thorough disinfecting between batches of crickets, throwing away any of the used paper "furnishings."

Where to get live food

The most convenient source of live insects for most people will be the local pet store. Any store that carries reptiles and reptile supplies should also have crickets and mealworms for sale in a variety of sizes. You can also buy live crickets and mealworms online. This can be a more economical option if you're buying them in large quantities, but unless you have an especially large colony you won't be buying enough for the savings to be significant. You can also find grasshoppers for sale online, as well as a wide array of other beetles and worms. You want to avoid getting too many fatty worms, like waxworms, but any variety of beetles and moths are suitable food for gliders, and an occasional foray into the online insect food world could be a great way to add more variety to your pet's protein diet. If you want to sample a few of a specific insect species to make sure your sugar gliders like them before getting too many, you can see if there's a reptile expo coming up anywhere nearby. Many companies that breed feeder insects do so with reptile owners in mind, and you'll often find at least a few insect breeders selling their wares at these events, in smaller quantities than you may be able to get online.

If you live in an area where crickets or grasshoppers are prevalent, it can be tempting to want to supplement your sugar glider's food with some free bugs from the backyard. Generally speaking, you should avoid doing this. Even if you don't use any pesticides in your own backyard, you can never be sure where the little guy was hopping before he got there. Most wild animals also carry a wide array of internal or external parasites, which can be transferred to your sugar glider. There's no reason to panic if your pets nab an occasional wild bug while they're out of their cage, but it's not a good idea to make a habit of feeding wild-caught insects to your sugar glider. The captive bred insects sold specifically for food through pet stores and online vendors will be much safer in the long run.

Staple food

In addition to the proteins, fruits, and vegetables your sugar gliders are offered once a day, there should be some sort of staple food made available to them 24/7. Refill and replace the dish as part of your daily cage maintenance, offering one tablespoon of staple food per two sugar gliders. While you want to be sure your sugar gliders are eating all of their protein and veggies, it's not important for them to eat all of their staple diet. Leftovers in the dish just mean they filled up on the healthier food you gave them at dinner time. The staple food is mostly there to keep up with the sugar glider's active metabolism, and you may even see your pets munching on it during the daytime, if they wake up in the middle of their night feeling peckish.

It is unlikely you'll find a suitable insectivore diet in your local pet shop. Your best bet for finding a solid

24-hour food for your sugar glider is to look online. Exotic Nutrition's Berries & Bugs diet is made from exactly that: gut-loaded larva, meat, and fruit. Florida-based breeder SunCoast Sugar Gliders makes a chicken and brown rice blend pelleted food that's popular with North American keepers. Zookeeper's Secret insectivore fare, also occasionally called Zoo-Fare, is another popular staple diet. Monkey biscuits, designed to suit the nutritional needs of both primates and marsupials, are another potential food source. While this might seem like a limited list, you should use caution when straying from these specific brands. Because they're still a relatively recent addition to the pet trade, very few companies are dedicated to making high-quality food for sugar gliders. If you find a new brand you're curious about, run it by your vet or the members of an online sugar glider forum to get their opinion before feeding it to your pets.

Easy meal recipes

On especially busy days, you might not have time to prepare your sugar glider's meal, and if you're going on vacation, your pet-sitter might find it tricky following the day-by-day diet plan you normally provide to your gliders. Most keepers like to mix up a pre-made diet and keep it in the freezer for these occasions.

With all of these recipes, you should thoroughly chop all larger ingredients in a food processor then combine them together and freeze them. To make it easier to portion the meal out at feeding time, you can freeze it into individual servings in ice cube trays. Put two tablespoons of the mixture into each cell of the tray—this will be enough for one meal for two gliders. When feeding time comes around, you can put the frozen meal-cicle right into the glider's dish. This style of meal can be used to substitute for a meal or two on your weekly diet plan, but should not be relied upon every day for an extended period of time—remember, variety is key to a healthy, happy glider.

Keep in mind, too, what was said about making all changes to a sugar glider's diet gradual. If you know you'll be going on vacation and will be having your gliders fed on pre-made diets while you're gone, you should start preparing for this a couple weeks in advance. Gradually introduce the pre-made diet as part of the glider's regular rotation. If you usually use it just one day a week, increase that to 3 or 4 in the couple of weeks just before you leave. This will make the switch to daily meal-cicles less jarring for your glider when you do leave.

There are a few popular recipes for these kinds of glider meal replacements, the most common of which are described below.

Taronga Zoo diet

This well-known captive glider diet was designed by a zookeeper to supplement a diet of fresh vegetables and insects. At the center of this recipe is an ingredient called Leadbeater's mixture, a nectar replacement made from 150ml of warm water, 150ml of honey, 1 shelled hard-boiled egg, 25 grams of a high-protein baby cereal, and 1 teaspoon of Vionate supplement. Leadbeater's mixture can also be used independently of the Tarnoga Zoo diet as a nutritional supplement added to the glider's daily protein (1 teaspoon per glider).

The recipe for Taronga Zoo diet is as follows:

- 3 grams each of apple, banana, sweet potato, and blueberries or kiwi
- 1.5 grams of sugar glider chow (any of the insectivore diets above will work)

- 1 teaspoon fly pupae (you can substitute crushed freeze-dried mealworms for this)

- 2 teaspoons of Leadbeater's mixture

- 4 grams orange

- 2 grams pear

Mix up the Leadbeater's mixture first; excess of that can also be frozen. Then, mix all ingredients in the recipe together in a food processor and freeze the resultant mixture.

The Pet Glider diet

An update and variant on the Taronga Zoo diet, the Pet Glider (a breeder website and online glider community - http://www.thepetglider.com/) has come up with this sugar glider diet for busy days that can be stored in the freezer for up to a month. Because it is more thorough in containing a variety of fruits, meats, and nutrients, this diet is perhaps the best to rely on for an extended period of time (like when you have a pet sitter during a vacation). The recipe is as follows:

- 1 cup (8 ounces) fresh or frozen fruit; choose four different types (1/4 cup each) from the following list: bananas, blueberries, cantaloupe, cherries, kiwi, mangoes, orange, papaya, peaches, pineapple, raspberries, strawberries, or tangerine. If using frozen, the fruit should contain no added sugar, spices, or other flavorings.

- 1 cup (8 ounces) fresh or frozen vegetables; choose four different types (1/4 cup each) from the following list: beets, bok choy, broccoli, carrots, cauliflower, collard greens, jicama, kale, lima beans, peas, red bell pepper, snow peas, squash, or sweet potatoes. Like with the fruits, make sure there's no added flavorings or sauces, especially when using frozen.

- 6 ounces plain full-fat yogurt with no artificial sweeteners
- 3 ounces calcium-fortified orange juice concentrate
- 2-3 ounces uncooked oatmeal
- 4 cups (32 ounces) unsweetened applesauce with no extra flavorings
- 6 ounces of cooked chicken, turkey, or eggs; eggs can be scrambled or boiled, turkey or chicken can be boiled, broiled, roasted, or pan-cooked in a small amount of extra virgin olive oil
- 1 tablespoon ground flax or wheat germ

Stir everything together except the oatmeal, then add the oatmeal a little at a time until the mixture has the consistency of cake batter. Sprinkle ¼ teaspoon of a multi-vitamin, like Vionate, on each ice cube serving. You can do this either before freezing or just before serving, just stay consistent so you don't over supplement (or forget to add it).

SunCoast Concoction

SunCoast Sugar Gliders (http://www.sugar-gliders.com/) is a large and well-known sugar glider breeder based out of Florida that has been mentioned before for their pre-made sugar glider chow. A great and knowledgeable source for all things glider, they've also come up with a quick meal recipe that they call their "concoction," which is what they feed to their gliders on busy days and recommend for those buying their animals.

The SunCoast concoction has the simplest recipe of the three suggested here, consisting of 1 ounce cooked white meat chicken, 1 tablespoon of plain or vanilla yogurt (full fat, no artificial sweeteners), 1 tablespoon of applesauce, and a pinch each of Vionate and RepCal. This is a smaller recipe, also, but can be expanded in this same ratio and can be stored in the freezer for up to a month.

Nutritional supplements

The use of supplements is a source of some debate in the sugar glider community. Most keepers will tell you they're not only helpful but necessary in the long-term health of captive sugar gliders. Others will say the dangers of over supplementing aren't worth the risk. While it's true that some vitamins and minerals can accumulate in the body, in most cases some kind of supplement is necessary to round out the sugar glider's nutrition. You'll notice all of the pre-made diets above—which were formulated by experienced breeders and zookeepers—contain some kind of supplement.

Calcium supplements are the most necessary to the health and longevity of sugar gliders. The ideal calcium to phosphorus ratio in a sugar glider diet is at least 2:1, something that can be difficult to achieve in a captive diet. Since these kinds of supplements are most commonly used in captive reptile diets, you're more likely to find them in the reptile and amphibian section than the small animal section of your pet store. If you can't find them there, you can buy them online. Rep-Cal is the most recommended brand of calcium supplement because all of their calcium supplements are phosphorus-free. The green label is best, but if you can only find the pink or white labels, they'll work too. The difference between them is that green label is straight calcium while the pink and white labels contain extra vitamin D3—not as necessary for gliders as it is for reptiles, though it also won't harm them and can help aid in the absorption of calcium.

Some keepers are wary of giving reptile calcium supplements to a mammal; the main argument goes that sugar gliders are a part of the family and deserve a "human grade" supplement. When it comes to calcium supplements, this is an unfounded concern so long as nothing except vitamin D3 has been added. These supplements are designed for use with pets that are just as much a part of their owner's family as the sugar glider is a part of yours, and the same safety and health precautions are being taken.

When it comes to mult-vitamin supplements, on the other hand, you don't want to give sugar gliders anything designed for reptiles—or humans, for that matter. Some breeders make and sell their own vitamin supplements, and though you should verify with your vet (or an online sugar glider forum) that these products are high-quality and safe, these are often well-formulated to take care of a sugar glider's needs. If you're looking for a commercial supplement, you can't go wrong with Vionate. Designed by veterinarians, this supplement has a mix of 21 vitamins and minerals that are necessary for the health of small animals, birds, and other pets.

If your sugar gliders are breeding, you may also want to consider adding a milk-replacement product to the diet of any pregnant or lactating females. Look for one designed for possums or marsupials, and make sure it doesn't contain any soy and has at least 20% protein. Both Exotic Nutrition (http://www.exoticnutrition.com/) and SunCoast Sugar Gliders http://www.sugar-gliders.com/) sell products specifically designed for use with sugar gliders.

Giving supplements

Mixing supplement powders into your gliders' food is generally the most effective means of delivering these nutrients. You should give each glider 1/8 of a teaspoon total of vitamins per day—about a pinch each of calcium and multi-vitamin supplement. For lactating females, you can add an extra 1/8 teaspoon of milk supplement. If it's a day you're giving your gliders yogurt or applesauce, the supplements will dissolve into the food easily and their somewhat bitter taste should be completely overpowered by the sweetness. You can also mix them into the day's chopped fruits and vegetables, or coat the bodies of feeder insects "shake and bake" style by putting the supplement into a plastic bag and dropping the day's insects in the bag to coat them just before feeding. Though there's nothing to dilute the taste in that case, insects are such a beloved treat of gliders that they'll be eager to eat the crickets or mealworms anyway.

Don't add the supplement powder to the staple food. Mostly this is to make sure they're getting the full complement of daily vitamins they need—the staple food is there as a back-up and you can't be sure all your gliders will eat all their alotted amount every day. Similarly, you should not add supplements to your glider's water bottle. Aside from concerns that they won't drink the whole bottle every day, the supplements contain compounds that can cause bacterial growth inside the bottle that could make your gliders sick. The bitter taste could also prevent the sugar gliders from wanting to drink their water, leading to dehydration.

Very rarely, the taste of the supplement powder on their food will make certain sugar gliders reject it. If this happens, you can try dissolving the supplement into a small amount of apple juice or nectar, which the glider should drink willingly. You could also make fortified suggie treats by mixing one teaspoon each of Vionate and Rep-Cal (or a similar calcium supplement) into 4 cups (32 ounces) of 100% fruit juice or fruit nectar. Apple juice and pear nectar seem to be particularly beloved by gliders. Pour the mixture two tablespoons at a time into ice cube trays and freeze. Like with the glider diets, give one cube per two gliders.

Nectar replacement diets

While it's true that sugar gliders are often sap-suckers in the wild, they mostly turn to this source of food when insects aren't as plentiful, and they prefer an insect-based diet if given the choice. Most keepers do not give their gliders a nectar supplement as part of their daily diet in captivity. Where these products can be helpful, however, is in administering supplements if your gliders are proving picky or refusing to eat any other form of diet supplementation. The sweet taste of the nectar replacement should entice the gliders. It can also be a helpful recovery food for sugar gliders suffering from calcium deficiency or Metabolic Bone Disease.

The three most popular nectar replacement diets are Suggie Soup, HPW diet, and the PML mixture. Recipes of all three are listed below. Keep in mind that these are special occasion diets and should not be fed to every glider every day. They are especially helpful in increasing the caloric consumption of breeding sugar gliders, helping the recovery of sick animals, or bulking up underweight individuals. Remember, if your sugar glider is lethargic, dragging its back legs, or showing other signs of calcium deficiency and illness, he should immediately be taken to the veterinarian. Nectar supplement diets can be an important part of a recovery program, but any such program should be arranged with your vet's help. If you don't have the time or resources to make your own nectar replacement, you can buy instant versions from Exotic

Nutrition (http://www.exoticnutrition.com/) and select sugar glider breeders.

Suggie Soup

Designed by the Lucky Glider Rescue & Sanctuary (http://www.luckyglider.org/) for rehabilitating animals, Suggie Soup is a low-fat, low-cholestrol, high calcium, and high protein recipe meant to deliver concentrated nutrition to ailing or breeding gliders. It can be fed as-is or diluted with water to be syringe fed to especially ill animals. For those who can eat on their own, you can freeze it into two tablespoon servings in ice cube trays like other sugar glider diets, although in this case—since the aim is recovery—a single glider should receive a whole two tablespoon serving.

To prepare Suggie Soup:

1) Scramble 1 small egg

2) Combine 1 tablespoon of bee pollen and 1 tablespoon of dehydrated fly pupae (or freeze-dried mealworms) in the blender and pulverize into a fine powder

3) Warm 2 cups of honey in the microwave or in a hot water bath on the stovetop. Don't use raw or comb honey—what you're looking for is a variety whose label says "filtered" or "pasteurized."

4) Once the honey's warm, mix it with 1 cup of canned mango juice and 1 cup of canned papaya juice. You can also liquefy fresh mango or papaya in a blender and use those.

5) Mix 1 tablespoon of a small animal protein supplement, like ZooPro or Wombaroo, into ¼ cup of plain, low-fat yogurt, then blend this into the juice and honey mixture along with the powdered mixture from step 2.

HPW Diet

Standing for "high protein wombaroo," HPW diets are approved for ailing marsupials of all stripes. The diet is similar to but simpler than the Suggie Soup described above. To make HPW diet:

1) Scramble 3 eggs and set aside to cool

2) Warm 2 cups of filtered honey in a microwave or warm water bath

3) Stir ¼ cup of a small animal protein supplement into the warm honey until it's dissolved together

4) Put the scrambled eggs, honey mixture, and 1 tablespoon of bee pollen into a blender and combine for 2-4 minutes, or until the mixture is smooth.

Serve it the same way as the Suggie Soup above. When frozen, it'll have the consistency of ice cream. Serve it alongside offered fruits, vegetables, and insects.

PML Mixture

PML stands for Pocket's Modified Leadbeaters, and is an alteration of the Leadbeater's formula described in the Turanga Zoo diet above. It was created by Des Hackett, who was one of the first individuals to devise a successful captive breeding program for both sugar gliders and the Leadbeater's possum, an endangered Australian species for whom the formula is named.

PML mixture is extremely similar to the HPW recipe described above. To make it:

1) Scramble 2 eggs and set aside to cool

2) Heat 14 ounces (1 ¾ cups) of water in the microwave for two minutes

3) Mix in an equal amount of honey, stirring until it dissolves

4) Add the diluted honey, eggs, and 1 ounce of a high-protein supplement to a blender and blend for 1 minute at a time until smooth.

Because it's more diluted than the above recipes,

PML mixture will be thinner and easier to administer

through an oral syringe for sick and injured animals. If

being given to breeding animals, you should serve it

alongside a smattering of fruit, vegetable, and insect

offerings. Like the above recipes, you should keep the

mixture frozen—the protein supplement will begin to

break down in as little as 4 days if kept in the

refrigerator. Feed 1-2 tablespoons to the animal per

day as directed by your vet.

Water

Fresh water should be made constantly available

to your sugar gliders. Refill the water bottles on a

daily basis, and empty, clean, and refill your water

bottles once a week to prevent build up of any

bacterial growth. It's best to use filtered water

whenever possible. Chemicals added to most tap

water to clean and fortify it for human consumption can give the water a funny taste to small animals, sometimes causing them to reject it. There's not yet ample data to determine what these chemicals can do to sugar gliders if fed in the long term, or if they can accumulate inside the body's systems, but suffice to say a simple home water filtration system is the best way to keep your glider's water healthy. One water bottle should work in cages with only two sugar gliders, but for larger colonies you'll want to provide at least two drinking locations within the enclosure.

Cleaning and cage maintenance

There are three main categories you have to think about when you're doing cage maintenance: the litter or bedding, the cage furnishings, and the cage itself. It's best to set up a daily, weekly, and monthly cleaning schedule and keep to it. When you're figuring out what supplies to use in your cleaning process, remember that sugar gliders are very scent-driven, and they'll be put off and irritated by unfamiliar odors, especially if they're permeating the whole cage from your cleaning. Use unscented soaps and laundry detergents whenever possible when you're cleaning the enclosure.

Disinfecting

There are occasions where a thorough disinfecting of the cage or its furnishings is required. This is especially important after a parasite infestation or other illness to make sure all traces are gone and won't re-infect your animals. In this situation, it's recommended to throw away any disposable bedding or litter, or any cage furnishings that are made of paper or wood—the eggs of some parasite species can survive inside these items for a surprisingly long time and are often too small to see. Smaller cage furnishings can be soaked in a solution of 10% bleach in warm water, then rinsed with clean water until all of the bleach odor is gone. In the case of cloth items, like sleeping and bonding pouches, you'll want to machine wash them following the disinfecting soak.

Because sugar glider cages are so large, disinfecting the entire cage can be a daunting challenge, but since gliders utilize every surface of the cage's interior it's important to be thorough. You can fill a simple plastic spray bottle, like a plant mister, with some of the bleach solution you've prepared, then wipe the bars down thoroughly with clean, warm water—again, until the bleach smell goes away. It's important that your gliders are secured in their secondary enclosure while you're doing this so they're not exposed to any of the cleaning solution.

Daily cage maintenance

You should make it a habit to check in on your gliders every day. Not only will this allow you to maintain an ideal clean environment, but it will also help you get used to the daily habits and behaviors of your gliders so you can notice any abnormalities as soon as they develop. Daily interaction is also the best way to keep your animals socialized and responsive to your touch.

Your daily maintenance should start with a spot-cleaning of any pelleted beddings or litters you're using. If you're using cage liners, change out the paper towel underneath and check the liner for solid waste. In cages with lots of gliders (or especially messy gliders) you'll likely need to change the entire liner on a daily basis. As far as other toys and furnishings, you should give them a look-over and wipe of any major spills or messes. Most gliders won't go to the bathroom in the bag they sleep in, but you should feel other cloth furnishings to make sure there're no wet spots.

Remove and empty the staple food dish. If it's been soiled in, also clean and dry the dish before refilling it. You should also check all water bottles, making sure that they're full. Press your finger against the tip after you've refilled it and before returning it to the cage to make sure there're no air bubbles blocking the flow. You should also give your gliders a serving of fruits and/or veggies and a serving of protein every day. Any used food dishes should be washed daily.

As far as when you perform all of these tasks, that's mostly dependent upon your schedule, but it's a good idea to be consistent. It's generally best to feed your gliders in the evening, which is when they'd normally start foraging in the wild. Because they're so naturally curious, many keepers find it easiest to do daily cage upkeep either while the gliders are out playing or while they're asleep during the daytime;

otherwise, you'll spend half the cleaning time fending off inquisitive suggies.

Weekly cage maintenance

If you're using pelleted litters or recycled paper bedding, you'll want to completely dispose of and replace it once every week. You should also thoroughly wash your water bottles every week, emptying them and running them through the dishwasher before returning them to use. You should also do a load of sugar glider laundry every week. This includes any used cage liners, sleeping or bonding pouches, and any scraps of fleece or other cage furnishings made of cloth. Other toys should also be removed and cleaned on a weekly basis with soapy water.

Monthly cage maintenance

Completely empty and clean the cage on a monthly basis. This is an expansion of your regular weekly cleaning tasks, as it includes all of the tasks under the weekly cleaning heading—emptying and disposing of used litter, cleaning all toys, and laundering all fabric furnishings. During monthly cleaning, though, you also want to wash the entire interior of the cage with warm, soapy water, making sure to get behind and underneath any permanent cage furnishings, like ledges, ramps, and branches. It's a good idea to also disinfect the litter pan while it's empty if your cage uses one, or at least give it a good thorough scrub—even though the gliders don't come into direct contact with it, it's the most likely place for mold or bacteria to develop.

Grooming

While their cages are notoriously messy, sugar gliders are typically fairly self-sufficient when it comes to personal grooming. Since only un-neutered males are known to have any kind of odor, they shouldn't require regular bathing. If you do need to bathe them, fill a sink with about 1 inch of warm water and use a gentle cat shampoo. This should only need to be done in very rare circumstances—if they get into something sticky or muddy, for example, or following a household flea infestation. If your sugar glider smells bad, don't instantly turn to bathing it unless you're sure it's from an external source. Bad odor emanating from a sugar glider can be a sign of serious health issues and you should call your vet.

How to trim Sugar Glider nails

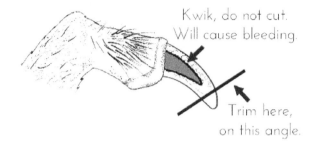

Kwik, do not cut.
Will cause bleeding.

Trim here,
on this angle.

Nail trimming

In the wild, a sugar glider's nails are worn down by walking over rocks and tree trunks in their natural habitat. If you want to avoid having to trim your glider's nails as often, you can simulate this within the captive environment. Trim track inserts for your running wheel are a great way to help your suggie's nails stay filed down. Don't use it all the time or it may injure the pads of your pets' paws. Just put it in when you notice your glider's nails getting a bit long— about once a month usually does it. You can also get

Lava Ledges or similar products and install them in the cage full-time. These are chew-safe jumping platforms designed to help trim small animal nails and cost around $5-$10 each. Put one or two in the area around the food dish, where your gliders will be guaranteed to go every day, and you'll rarely—if ever—have to trim their nails yourself.

The easiest way to trim a glider's nails is to put them into their bonding pouch or sleeping pouch, holding them down gently while you draw out one limb at a time. You can use a pair of cat claw trimmers to actually trim the nail. When you look at your glider's toe, you'll see a spot on the nail where it changes color. This is where the quick starts, the part of the nail that hurts and will bleed when trimmed. It's better to trim a little bit at a time than to trim too much. If you do nick the quick, you can stop the bleeding with some flour or cornstarch. Once that's stopped, rinse the nail and put a dab of antiseptic ointment on it, then watch it to make sure it doesn't develop an infection.

Play time

The most fun part of your daily care routine is, of course, when you get to play with your sugar gliders. Even when they're given a large enclosure and plenty of toys, sugar gliders need to be let out to roam as often as possible to get ample exercise. Out of cage time also gives you the best chance to interact with your sugar gliders.

Since they're nocturnal, sugar gliders are going to be most active after the sun goes down. Some sugar gliders adapt to their keepers' schedule, but most will be sleepy and less likely to be social if you're interacting with them during the day. How they react to play time is largely dependent on the personality of your individual animals. Some will be constantly in motion, jumping from the curtains to the houseplants, and back. Others will want to ride around on your shoulder and snuggle up with their humans, regardless of the time of day. As with most advice given to keepers of exotic animals, you'll get the best results by tailoring your playtime to your pet's natural instincts.

Safe play spaces

Even if your sugar gliders are all fairly mellow, you want to be careful to glider-proof any room you let them out to play in. They're fast critters with a natural instinct to find any available hiding space. If possible, it's best to avoid letting them out to play in a kitchen area, simply because of the multitude of dangerous places they can get themselves into. If they are in a kitchen, make sure there're no glider-sized gaps around or behind the cabinets and that they can't get under or behind the fridge, stove, or any other appliance. Bathrooms can also be tricky. Make sure the lid of the toilet is closed—sugar gliders can easily fall in but won't be able to climb the porcelain to get out and may drown. Also make sure all drains are stoppered and any cleaning products or medicines are stashed carefully away.

With any room you let your gliders out to play in, take a second to look around the space with your pet's eyes before letting them out to explore. Check both up high and down low for open heating vents, radiators, or gaps in the baseboard. Make sure there're no open windows or pet doors they can squeeze through and get outside. While they're not as naturally destructive as rodents, sugar gliders may chew on cords or wires. It's nearly impossible to remove all the power cords from a room, but make sure there're no areas they could chew without you seeing them, like behind an entertainment center or underneath a desk. Make sure to carefully supervise your sugar gliders when they're outside the cage, especially the first few times you let them out in a space. You're almost guaranteed to have missed at least one hiding spot, and your pets are almost guaranteed to find it. So long as you're supervising them, you can find and fix these areas for the next playtime.

It's generally not advisable to take your sugar gliders outside without a bonding pouch. Between their speed, their curiosity, and their ability to hide, a glider can wander off and out of sight before you have a chance to catch it.

Dealing with bites

While a well-kept sugar glider is not likely to bite often, it will happen occasionally and is something you should be prepared for while you're interacting. Sugar gliders bite for a number of reasons. Primarily, they'll bite when they feel threatened or scared. This is most common to experience when you're first bringing a sugar glider home, and should stop once you've built up trust.

Sugar gliders that are just maturing into adulthood are also known to bite more frequently than other animals. You can see this as a kind of teenage rebellion. This is the time in a sugar glider's life when it would normally be determining its place in the hierarchy of the colony, and maturing sugar gliders have been known to bite their keepers with no other signs of aggression, completely out of the blue, as if testing how they'll react. There's not a whole lot you can do to curb this behavior aside from using a sleeping pouch or piece of fleece over your hand when handling your glider until the phase plays itself out. The behavior rarely lasts longer than a month or two.

Most bites from a well-socialized sugar glider are either exploratory or—believe it or not—a sign of affection. If your hands have a different smell than usual, especially if you've recently been eating a tasty snack, your gliders may nip or lick your fingers hoping to find a treat. Sweet-smelling lotions or perfumes are also likely to draw unwanted nibbles. In these situations, offering them an actual treat will often distract them from the biting. While this may seem to you like reinforcing bad behavior, your sugar glider's mind will not attach receiving the treat with biting a finger, but rather with the good smell it was already expecting to be food. Remember that sugar gliders are still relatively wild animals. You won't be able to train it not to bite something it thinks it can eat, and your best bet is not to smell like food at all. Love nips or grooming nips will have a very similar set of lead-up behaviors to exploratory bites, including licking and nuzzling. Again, the best bet is often to distract them with food or a treat. However much a bite hurts, what they're trying to tell you is that they consider you a member of the colony—and that's certainly not something you want to discourage.

Sugar gliders are not aggressive and as a rule won't bite or attack without cause. Rescued sugar gliders may display seemingly aggressive behaviors, learned over a lifetime of abuse and neglect, but if a well-socialized animal is frequently biting people you should assume he's got a reason. If more than one glider in the colony is acting out, there could be an issue with the environment that's making them feel threatened. Make sure the cage is large enough, they're provided adequate stimulation, and they have places to sleep and hide. If there are other people in the household, make sure no one else is mishandling or mistreating the animals, causing them to lash out at you. Frequent unprompted defensive bites could also be a sign of hidden injury and illness, and if you can't find another cause, it's a good idea to make an appointment with your vet. Even if there's nothing wrong, she can give you some pointers on what's causing the behavior.

If you are bitten, the most important thing to do is to stay calm. Sugar glider bites hurt—their teeth tear through tree bark and are perfectly capable of breaking the skin, possibly (though rarely) requiring stitches. As difficult as it can be to do, the most important thing is to not pull your hand away too fast. This will trigger the glider's instincts and may prompt them to bite again. Slowly draw the bitten area away from the glider. Wash the area with antibacterial soap, apply antibiotic ointment, and cover it with a Band-Aid while you determine if the bite is serious enough to require medical attention.

Chapter 5: Health, Wellness, and Breeding

Prevention is key when it comes to maintaining your sugar glider's health. They are hardy animals and not prone to developing any illnesses or ailments, provided they receive proper nutrition and care. In fact, the majority of ailments listed later in this chapter are completely preventable through adequate nutrition. This is an important thing to keep in mind because you won't be able to tell right away if there's a problem with your glider's diet. Like many prey species, sugar gliders in the wild are accustomed to hiding any signs of illness or injury. Sick animals are typically the first to be picked off by predators, and gliders have an instinctual aversion to showing signs of weakness. This is fabulous for survival in the wild, but means you can't count on your pets to let you know when something's wrong—and by the time they do, it often means serious damage has already been done.

Sugar gliders aren't known to carry any disease and don't require any vaccinations upon first bringing them home. Early-life vet expenses are likely to include only the initial check-up and neutering for any non-breeding males. With good nutrition, gliders are not as prone to cancer or other issues as they age as other small animals.

Finding a vet

If the breeder where you bought your animal is close to where you live, they may be the best source of information on the closest place for you to find an exotic animal vet. Not all veterinarians will know how to care for sugar gliders, and though some may be willing to learn, it's best to look for a vet who's at least accustomed to treating exotic animals in general, if not sugar gliders in particular.

The Sugar Glider Help website (http://www.sugargliderhelp.com) lists about 650 sugar glider veterinarians in North America, searchable in their database. While you'll need to see a vet in person for surgical procedures and check-ups, the site also lists some vets willing to make consultations over the phone or the internet, if there's an emergency and you need advice sooner than you can make the trip.

The typical vet visit for a sugar glider check-up is around $50-$100. Most will do a nail trimming for around $5-10 per animal. More advanced or complicated procedures vary wildly, but rarely cost more than $500.

Neutering

Neutering is recommended for male sugar gliders unless you expressly plan to breed them. Not only is it the best way to prevent unwanted pregnancies in a mixed-gender colony, but it can also curb defensive and territorial behaviors in your male gliders. Neutering can be done surgically or with lasers. Surgical procedures are more invasive and require more post-surgery recovery, and tend to cost around $50-$100 per animal. Not every vet will have the equipment to perform laser surgeries; if they do, the procedure's more expensive (up to $350 per animal) but significantly less invasive.

Sugar gliders can be neutered as young as four months out of pouch. If you're keeping the male in an enclosure with females—especially its parents or siblings—you absolutely want to neuter the animal before it reaches sexual maturity, which occurs around nine months out of pouch. Even if there're no females living in the house, if you find your male sugar gliders are fighting for dominance, neutering one or both of them should solve the problem.

Signs of a problem

The sugar glider's aforementioned propensity for hiding illness makes identifying problems difficult, but there are some signs you can look out for to help spot issues early. Changes to the glider's fur can be a sign of a skin problem, an external parasite, or an issue with the diet. With the exception of un-neutered males (who will have a bald spot in the center of their forehead) there should be no bald or thin patches in a sugar glider's fur. The fur should be sleek and unbroken, without "cracks" or spots that it seems to separate. New and unpleasant body odor is also a sign of a problem and should be cause for concern. If the glider is trembling or shaking when it's not showing any other signs of fear, that's a symptom of anemia, malnutrition, or calcium deficiency, and should be immediate cause to call your vet.

Other signs of a problem are similar to those in other small mammals. Drooping ears, drooping eyes, eyes that are half-shut, or discharge from the eyes, ears, or nose are all signs of infection. Listlessness and depression are also causes for concern, as is dehydration. You can tell if your animal is dehydrated by doing a "pinch test." Sugar glider skin should have a similar elasticity to that of humans. If you gently pinch the skin on their back into a peak and then let it go, it should regain its usual shape almost immediately. If it doesn't, the animal is dehydrated. Call your vet, and if your animal can't be seen right away, give it some pediatric electrolyte solution. You can use an oral syringe if it won't drink on its own.

Common health ailments

The most common issues with sugar glider health tend to be connected to a poor diet. These include malnutrition, calcium deficiency, dental issues, and obesity. Other common causes for visits to the vet are injury, infections, and stress disorders.

Metabolic Bone Disorder

Afflicting a wide range of small animals, Metabolic Bone Disorder—also called nutritional osteodystrophy—is the result of long-term calcium deficiency. It can be caused either by a diet lacking in calcium or too high in phosphorus, which blocks the absorption of calcium by the body. Metabolic Bone Disorder is a serious ailment that causes distortions to the skeletal structure, most frequently manifesting in the limbs and face. Signs of MBD include spontaneous bone fractures, bulging along the jaw or cheeks, or new and unnatural curvatures of the spine. In severe cases, it may result in partial paralysis, causing your gliders to drag one or both rear limbs.

MBD is entirely preventable with proper nutrition and is also completely reversible if caught early enough. Call your vet right away if you notice any of the signs above. They'll likely recommend some dietary changes and additional supplements, and may put your pet on a regiment of Neocalglucon or Calciquid to help rebuild calcium quickly.

Nutritional problems

Sugar gliders that don't get enough exercise are prone to obesity. This can also be caused by a diet that's too high in fats and sugars, or an imbalance in the gilder's fat to protein ratio. Just like with humans, obesity has long-term health consequences, including problems with the heart, liver, and pancreas.

On the other side of the nutritional spectrum, sugar gliders that don't get enough nutrients can become malnourished. Malnourished gliders are often weak, lethargic, and may have trouble walking. Trembling and seizures are signs of severe malnutrition. The results of a lacking diet can be low glucose and protein levels in the blood or problems producing red blood cells, and eventually can lead to liver or kidney failure.

Finally, issues with a sugar glider's teeth are most frequently caused by problems with their diet. Tooth problems can result from eating too many soft foods or food too high in carbohydrates. Advanced dental disease can lead to fractured or rotting teeth and tooth loss. They may paw at their mouth or refuse food if the problem gets bad enough. Your vet will typically check your glider's teeth as a part of its regular check-up. This is the best way to catch tooth problems before they become serious.

Infections and parasites

Many of the bacteria and parasites that infect sugar gliders are transmitted to them by other animals. If there are rabbits in the house, sugar gliders are susceptible to the *Pasteurella multocida* bacteria they carry. Households with cats should take great care to avoid having sugar gliders come into contact with cat droppings because they can cause toxoplasmosis, a parasitic disease that manifests as severe diarrhea and stomach problems, sometimes leading to fatal dehydration. Also use caution when handling your sugar gliders if any other animals in the house fall ill with cryptosporidiosis (crypto). This potentially deadly parasite can afflict both reptilian and mammalian species, and can also be contracted by humans. It at the least causes flu-like symptoms, and can be fatal if left untreated. They can also contract a number of familiar human bacteria, like staph and strep infections. Early signs of infection are similar to those of other illnesses: lethargy, loss of appetite, or sudden unexplained weight loss. Sugar gliders tend to react well to antibiotic treatment, and your vet will be able to prescribe something to get your pets back in perfect health.

Captive-born sugar gliders don't frequently have external parasites. Again, those they do contract are typically carried to them from other animals in the house. If your dog gets fleas, for example, you should probably check your gliders, replacing their litter or bedding and washing their fabric cage furnishings just in case. Mites, worms, and other parasites are very rare.

Stress injuries

Self-mutilation of the limbs, tails, or genitals is commonly seen in two groups: solitary animals and un-neutered males. This behavior may be accompanied by other stress behaviors, like pacing in front of the cage bars, overeating, over-drinking, and eating their own waste. If you have a single sugar glider, the only way to stop these behaviors is to buy your pet a companion. Males who do have companions that are displaying these behaviors will almost certainly stop once they've been neutered.

Any of these symptoms alone—and especially two or more together—are ways for your pets to tell you there's something stressing them out. Most often, this is a sign your gliders are under-stimulated. They need more playtime, more toys, or more interaction with their humans—or sometimes all three. It could also mean the enclosure's just too small. If your cage isn't at least 3 feet tall, buy a bigger one. If you have cats in the house, make sure they're not constantly watching the gliders when you're not in the room— they've been known to perch outside of cages all night and terrify the little guys. Keep an eye on how your animals are interacting with each other; dominance fights could be causing tension in the colony.

Breeding

As you can tell from the warnings about neutering males, getting your sugar gliders to mate is not the difficult part of breeding. Your primary concern is going to be maintaining the health of all your sugar gliders. Since they're housed communally, the greatest threat to the health of females is over-breeding. Though they only produce 1-3 joeys per litter, females can have up to 4 litters per year, and if you're not careful in making plans for what to do with the joeys once they're weaned, the care of a breeding colony can get overwhelming fast. Make sure you've given adequate thought to all of these concerns before starting any kind of breeding program, and absolutely take all breeding animals to the vet to get a clean bill of health before you start.

The advice that follows here is only a general overview of what to expect when you breed your gliders. If you are serious about breeding your animals, you should discuss it with your vet and do your own research, talking to established breeders either online or in person before you begin. Also keep the issue of legality in mind. The USDA doesn't require breeders with fewer than 4 breeding females to have a license, but the specific requirements of your area may be different. Be sure you check with your local Fish & Wildlife department before you start breeding so you don't risk losing all your animals.

Determining sexual maturity

It's easy to tell when male sugar gliders are ready to breed because of the diamond-shaped bald patch that will appear over the scent gland on their forehead. It's more difficult to tell with females. As a basic rule of thumb, it's not safe to breed a female who's younger than 7 months, and it's generally best to wait until they're over a year old to make sure they're fully mature.

Pregnancy and birth

Because they're marsupials, pregnant gliders can remain in the enclosure with their colony. Pregnant females should be given more protein than your average sugar glider—a milk replacement product can be useful for this, or some of the nectar replacement diets outlined in chapter 4. If you notice the other gliders in the enclosure getting chubby from eating the pregnant female's diet, you can give it to her during out of cage play time as a treat.

The gestation period for sugar gliders is incredibly short—around 2-3 weeks in a standard pregnancy. After that, the infant remains in the pouch for 2-3 months before emerging into the nest. You can leave the glider with her colony during this process, but it's generally best for you as a keeper to leave her alone while she's got a joey in the pouch. This will avoid undue stress or accidental injury to the developing joey.

Joeys in the nest

Joeys emerge from the pouch small and hairless, with their eyes still closed. At around three weeks out of pouch, the joeys will open their eyes and begin to wean. This is the point at which it's safe to start gently handling the joeys, although you should back off if the parents start crabbing or getting defensive—sugar gliders can be especially brutal if they're attacking in defense of their young. Unlike many wild animal species, males are involved in rearing and feeding the baby joeys, and it's safe—and in fact encouraged—to keep the family together in the same cage.

Newborns should eat semi-solid foods until they've been out of the pouch for about three months. Human baby food that's high in protein with no added preservatives can be great for joeys, too—sweet potato and chicken flavors seem especially beloved. Low-fat fruit-flavored yogurt can also be a great joey food. At around the three-month mark, you can start introducing adult foods, like mealworms and fruit or veggie mixes, to your joeys.

It's not only possible to handle the joeys once they open their eyes—it's necessary to get the pet accustomed to humans. This is a process known as "hand-gentling," and is what breeders use to teach gliders to bond with humans as well as others of their own kind. Each joey should receive daily handling and one-on-one bonding time with his human. If you don't have time to spend personal time with the joeys, you don't have time to breed your sugar gliders and shouldn't do it.

If you're planning on selling or otherwise re-housing the baby sugar gliders once they reach adulthood, it's a good idea to move them into a separate enclosure once they reach around 3 months of age. Shared playtime after this point is fine and will likely be welcomed, but this will start the separation process so it's not as stressful on either the joey or the parents once the full break happens.

It should also be noted that, rarely, females within a colony have been known to display aggressive behavior toward female joeys as they're reaching adulthood. For this reason, it's a good idea to have a secondary enclosure ready even if you don't plan on selling the babies. The sugar gliders can often be re-integrated into their home colony once they're fully grown, but could be seriously injured or even killed by aggressive displays from the adults as they're still growing.

Additional Resources

For additional reading, I recommend these internet forums & websites:

- Sugar Glider Help:

  http://www.sugargliderhelp.com/

- Suncoast Sugar Gliders: http://www.sugar-gliders.com/

- "Glider Gossip" Forum:

  http://www.sugarglider.com/

- Glider Central Forum:

  http://www.glidercentral.net/

Made in the USA
Middletown, DE
23 February 2020